Paul Roberts

May 2007

Midlands Bus Memories in Colour
By Paul Roberts

Copyright IRWELL PRESS Ltd.,
ISBN-10 1-903266-76-9
ISBN-13 978-1-903266-76-2
First published in 2007 by Irwell Press Ltd., 59A, High
Street, Clophill, Bedfordshire, MK45 4BE
Printed by Alden Press, Oxford.

Introduction

This book is a celebration of some of the multitude of bus operators in the east and west Midlands over a ten-year period beginning in the mid-1960s. I was born and bred in Doncaster and a fascination with buses inhabits even my earliest memories. This interest was helped by living only a few hundred yards from the Corporation Transport depot in a town that was served by no less than twenty bus companies, large and small.

In 1967 I started a new adventure by moving to college in Dudley. Every so often, armed with a Midland Red 'Day Anywhere Ticket' I was able to start exploring new areas. I was fascinated by all manner of operators; the proud municipals bearing their distinctive liveries and coats of arms, the large regional companies and the tremendous variety of independents ranging from Barton with a fleet of over 300 buses to Churchbridge with a few coaches and just one double-decker. This was also a time when many independents, particularly those in South Staffordshire, had a large proportion of second-hand buses bought from operators all over the UK – always a source of additional interest for the enthusiast. My father had nurtured my interest in photography throughout my formative years and it was only natural that I would attempt to record visits to operators, hardly imagining that this would become archive material for the 21st century. I would like to have recorded far more of these remarkable buses and fleets

but with colour slide film equivalent to a day's wages I had to be selective in my choice of subjects.

In 1969 I started as a part-time conductor, then became a driver for Harpers of Heath Hayes. Being let loose on such a selection of buses including RTs, RTLs, Royal Tigers, Guy Arabs, PD2s and PD3s just did not seem like work to an enthusiast. A major bus industry upheaval followed soon after my colour photography started, with the formation of the Passenger Transport Executives (PTEs) when numerous operators were absorbed. This provided further interest with many buses appearing in unfamiliar liveries. The first views are of buses in the Birmingham conurbation, continuing on a circular tour around the region and culminating in a look at operators in the East Midlands and the South-west of the area. I am indebted for help and support from several people, notably Paul Anderson, my mentor, and Ian Nicholls who scanned the ageing slides. Long forgotten facts were supplied by Mick Collins, Tony Hall, Dave Holt, Steve Page, Steve Poultney, Stuart Turner and Richard Weaver. I also thank my sister, Jane Caldwell for her early proof reading and my wife Dot for pushing me along at every stage.

Paul Roberts
Leicester, 2007

In 1968 Barton Transport acquired a pair of AEC Renowns with Park Royal H74F bodies which had previously been operated by Smiths of Barrhead, near Paisley, Glasgow. The second of the two, No.1116 (212 JUS) is at Barton's Ilkeston garage. Although two more second-hand double-deckers were purchased in the following year, Barton's operations were soon to be caught up in the bus grant revolution; all its double-deckers were replaced by the 'necessary specification' single-deck coaches on Leyland or Bedford chassis.

In 1949/50 Birmingham City Transport received 260 Crossley double-deckers. The first 160 had exposed radiators while the last 100 had modern looking 'tin fronts'. On 11 August 1965, no.2268 (JOJ 268) an all-Crossley DD42/6 with H30/24R bodywork, is travelling down Queensway from The Old Square on a one-way section of road. This was a period when Birmingham was reputed to change its one-way system on a weekly basis and indeed, Queensway was soon to become a conventional dual carriageway. The large building to the left of the picture is Lewis's department store. By 1965, 300 Daimler Fleetlines had been delivered to BCT and this chassis was to become a Birmingham standard throughout the 1960s. The example to the right of the picture has 72 seats available and will have little difficulty accommodating the long queue that stretches back alongside the new building development.

Birmingham City Transport was well known for its large fleet of 'Standards' with similar bodies on Crossley, Daimler, Leyland and Guy chassis. It also received 100 Leyland PD2s in 1949/1950 with half the batch being all-Leyland products and the other half having bodies built by Park Royal. One of the latter, No.2228 (JOJ 228) is waiting in Dudley bus station before returning to Birmingham on the 74 route, jointly operated with West Bromwich Corporation. The journey through to Birmingham was slower than that operated by BMMO (Midland Red) but was 1/6d (7½p) when the BMMO fare was 3/- (15p). This price differential was a good incentive to use the cheaper service. The two Midland Red buses in the background are in a drop-off and parking area and will move up the hill to the main bus station ready for loading just before their departure time.

The Midland Red Oldbury garage had a glass roof, giving it a light and airy feel and making photography relatively easy compared with many other premises. This 1974 view was taken soon after the sale to West Midland Passenger Transport Executive. The maroon ex-Coventry Daimler CVG6s, No.239Y (VWK 239) and No.240Y (VWK 240) have recently been transferred from their home city and make unusual stable-mates for the ex-Midland Red vehicles. Also visible to the right is a pair of BMMO D9s in their new West Midlands livery and a BMMO S17 and D9 still in red but carrying vinyls with their new owner's name and logo. The Alexander-bodied Daimler Fleetline to the left of No.240Y is also ex-Midland Red though it carries West Midlands livery. Another stranger in the camp can be seen through the cab of No.239Y, an ex-Birmingham City Transport Daimler Fleetline.

Soon after 413 Midland Red buses and their eight garages were transferred to West Midlands Passenger Transport Executive, vehicle availability was affected and ageing Birmingham 'Standards' were moved into the Black Country to assist with operations. This view of Oldbury garage in 1974 shows two 1952 ex-Birmingham Daimler CVG6s with Crossley H55R bodies. Just to the rear is an original resident, No.5023 (3023 HA), a BMMO D9 with H72RD BMMO bodywork, still in red but carrying a WM logo over the offside headlight. The two Daimlers, Nos.2787/8 (JOJ 787/8) were to soldier on to 1974/5 respectively, a fine tribute to post-war British engineering.

BMMO, the Birmingham and Midland Motor Omnibus Company Ltd, was better known as Midland Red. It built its own buses at Carlyle Road Works in Edgbaston for a period of 47 years. Their ultimate double-decker was the D9, with many advanced features for its time, including independent suspension, servo-assisted brakes and power steering. The BMMO-built 30ft long bodies had seats for 72 passengers. 345 D9s were built for service with the parent company between 1960 and 1966, but on 3 December 1973, just over a quarter of them were transferred to the West Midlands Passenger Transport Executive (WMPTE) fleet. Repaints in WMPTE colours started to appear fairly rapidly and one Sunday morning in 1974 found this splendidly posed line-up of alternative liveries on five D9s at Oldbury garage. Starting on the left is No.5321 (6321 HA), one of the first D9s to have its upstairs front hopper vents replaced by fixed windows. Next are No.5347 (6347 HA), No.5327 (6327 HA), No.5403 (BHA 403C) and finally No.5359 (6359 HA). No.5403 was amongst the last 45 built and had its bodywork finished by Willowbrook at Loughborough.

Dudley bus station must have been troublesome for drivers with its bus stops placed on steep gradients. Vehicles such as this pair of BMMO D7s with only 8.0 litre engines and crash gearboxes would have been stretched to the limit when pulling away up the hill with a full load. On this particularly snowy day in January 1968 there were few takers for the services of the 'Friendly Midland Red' and hopefully there will not be too much trouble coaxing them away up the snow-covered slope. These three buses are led by No.4729 (729 BHA) built in 1957 and carrying Metro-Cammell H58RD bodywork. The D9 at the rear has 10.5 litres at its disposal but with its semi-automatic transmission could possibly still have traction problems in these adverse weather conditions. In 1986 the bus station was rebuilt and the layout revised with most of the stops being moved to the level.

West Bromwich Corporation thought highly of Daimlers and all its half-cab double-deckers from pre-war days until 1969 came from the relatively local Coventry manufacturer. This Weymann H30/26R bodied CVG6 of 1952, No.172 (GEA 172) and one of a batch of twenty, is near the King's Cinema en route to Wednesbury, in 1969. It is about to be overtaken by an ERF lorry of 1960s vintage. An unusual feature of West Bromwich Corporation's buses was that the front seats downstairs were inward-facing, giving the conductor more space to manoeuvre.

West Bromwich Corporation buses carried a very traditional livery up to the delivery of their last six half-cab double-deckers in 1965. No.265 (CEA 265C) is the last of the batch and is carrying two-tone blue and cream complete with gold lining-out and traditional-style fleet name. All subsequent deliveries between 1968 and 1970 were rear-engined Daimler Fleetlines and carried a much-simplified livery of cream with light blue bands as can be seen on the rear of the bus on the extreme right. No.265 is a Daimler CVG6-30 with Metro-Cammell H41/33R bodywork and was delivered some time after the other five, having been fitted with an experimental ventilation system. As a result of this, air-inlet grills are fitted either side of the destination boxes and the bus has fixed side windows in the upper saloon with just a small quarter-light towards the rear.

Walsall Corporation Transport Willowbrook H36/34RD-bodied Sunbeam F4A No.852 (TDH 902) in difficulties in the Dudley Fields Estate. These trolleybuses were the first 30 foot two-axle buses to be permitted in the UK and 852 is the second in the batch of 22 vehicles delivered between 1954 and 1956. The AEC tower wagon has been called from the nearby Birchills garage and the crew are attending to a problem with the right-hand trolley boom. Meanwhile a handful of passengers patiently wait for the vehicle to return to service. This view was taken in 1969 before West Midlands Passenger Transport Executive took over Walsall Corporation Transport. The PTE continued to run the trolleybuses until 1970, although they removed the Walsall coat of arms and name. They never applied their own fleet names, running the trolleybuses anonymously until their final demise on Saturday 3rd October 1970.

Walsall Corporation ran trolleybuses until 1970 and had a large number of second-hand vehicles in its fleet. No.310 (BDY 819) is a 1947 Sunbeam W with Weymann H30/26R body originally operated by Maidstone & District and sold to Walsall in 1959. It is negotiating the turning circle at the Mossley Estate terminus. These buses were partially rebuilt at Walsall in the transport department workshops and the saloon windows were re-fitted with white rubber mountings, seen clearly here in the low winter sun. The long shadows of the author and his companion are evident in the snow-covered foreground.

Many independent operators purchased ex-London Transport RTLs and RTs in large numbers in the 1950s, as reliable replacements for ageing buses long past their best after the war. It was not so common for municipal fleets to buy them second-hand, but Walsall Corporation No.204 (OLD 601) is one of the five purchased in 1959. On Wednesday 1 October 1969 it is between duties in Walsall town centre, just opposite St Paul's bus station. This was the day on which the West Midlands Passenger Transport Executive was formed and Walsall Corporation Transport, along with all the other local municipal operators, was brought under the control of this new organisation.

Resplendent in its original Walsall Corporation blue livery and proudly carrying the town coat of arms is No.12 (2742 DH). It was one of a batch of 30 Daimler Fleetlines delivered between 1962 and 1965 with short 27ft 6in bodies and forward entrances built by Northern Counties but still managing to seat 70 passengers. They had other unusual features including white window rubbers, rounded fronts and fibreglass body panels rather than aluminium. They were designed to be conductor-operated until a conversion was made with a second door ahead of the front wheel, enabling the driver to collect the fares. The vehicle is in Dudley bus station in 1969 with the newly built Bird Cage Walk shopping Centre in the background. It is about to make the 25-mile journey to Stafford via Wednesbury, Walsall and Cannock.

Walsall Corporation Transport operated the longest and the shortest Daimler Fleetline buses in the UK. No.56 (XDH 56G) was the longest at 36 feet and was the only CRC6-36 to operate in Britain. It was originally displayed at the 1968 Earls Court Commercial Motor Show, in a unique light blue livery. Its Northern Counties body originally seated 86 passengers. It has two doors, one ahead of the front axle and the other at the very rear. It also has two staircases with a CCTV camera covering the rear-entrance, relaying the view to a monitor in the cab. At that time, it was illegal to have a TV monitor where it could be viewed by the driver, a far cry from today where multiple cameras can be relaying images constantly to a screen in the cab. The monitor had to remain switched-off until legislation was changed to accommodate this feature. No.56 was regularly used on route 118 Walsall to Birmingham and had a reputation for being unreliable. This is 1969 and it is appropriate that it is being towed into Birchills garage behind a Walsall AEC wrecker with '118-Walsall' still showing on the destination blind. This bus is now undergoing preservation as part of the BAMMOT collection at Wythall near Birmingham.

Walsall Corporation No.1 (1 UDH) is unique in being the shortest Daimler Fleetline double-decker built; only 25 feet long and with no front overhang gives it a similar appearance to a trolleybus. It is fitted with a single sliding door just behind the front wheels, and manages to squeeze 64 seated passengers into its Northern Counties body. It was originally delivered in Walsall Corporation blue livery but is seen here in the early 1970s soon after re-paint into West Midlands Passenger Transport Executive's blue and cream. It is entering Cannock bus station on the long route from Stafford to Dudley, a journey of 25 miles and over two hours duration.

This busy scene in Cannock bus station in 1974 shows No.3393 (393 KOV) a 1964 Daimler Fleetline Metro-Cammell H72F bodywork which is operating from the Walsall Birchills depot. The bus was originally bought by Birmingham City Transport and would not normally have ventured beyond the city boundary until take-over by West Midlands Passenger Transport Executive (WMPTE). BDJ 807, the ex-St Helens RT to the left in Harper Bros. green livery is about to make the twenty mile journey into Birmingham under the new ownership of Midland Red; therefore it is carrying an 853 route number in the cab window. Having reached their twilight years these ancient 56-seaters were called upon to do all-day service on the longest routes whilst newer buses were rushed off to Central Works to be re-painted into NBC poppy red. The distinctive rear-end of a WMPTE Bristol VR can also be seen entering the station.

This is 1971, soon after Wolverhampton Corporation Transport was absorbed into WMPTE. There are three liveries here, all on Guy Arab buses. No.571 (KJW 571) an Arab IV bodied by Roe is in Wolverhampton Corporation Transport green and cream, No.170 (GJW 170C) an Arab V with a Metro-Cammell H72F body, is in the standard early WMPTE colours featuring a Birmingham style khaki roof. Another Arab V on the right is in an early experimental version with a khaki roof and cream domes. The imposing Chubb lock and safe works fills the skyline to the right. The transport department Land Rover on the left was sometimes seen pulling broken-down buses back to the depot when a more suitable breakdown vehicle was unavailable, although it was on occasion seen to be somewhat taxed by a 30 foot double-decker.

Park Lane, Wolverhampton was well known for being the home of Guy Motors from 1914 until its sad demise in 1978. Directly opposite was the Park Lane Garage of Wolverhampton Corporation where one of the home products, No.560 (FJW 560), a Guy Arab III with Park Royal H54R bodywork, heads a line-up of five venerable open platform half-cabs. All of these buses will be required for service during the afternoon peak period. Clear signs of trolleybus operation can be seen in this view, after their withdrawal from this depot in January 1964. There are overhead supports in evidence although the valuable copper overhead wire has been removed.

Wolverhampton Corporation was one of the few municipals to operate beyond its borough boundary. This 1963 Guy Arab V No.142 (142 DDA) with Park Royal H72F bodywork is in the picturesque village of Brewood, a few miles to the north of Wolverhampton in the county of Staffordshire, in 1970. The fleet was taken over by the West Midlands Passenger Transport Executive that year and No.142 carries West Midlands fleet names but is still in the old Corporation green livery. Three years later Midland Red took over operation of the cross-boundary services from Wolverhampton. The route was re-numbered service 878 and was operated from its Cannock garage. The building to the left is Speedwell Castle, a folly dating back to the 1740s.

Colliery contracts were a useful source of income to operators large and small. The bus park at Lea Hall colliery near Rugeley was a typical scene, reflected at pits all round the country. The coach in the foreground is CDH 173L, a 1973 Duple Dominant-bodied Ford belonging to Central of Walsall, which sold out to West Midlands Passenger Transport Executive in 1984. Next in the line-up is a pair of Midland Red S23s built in 1969 in the company's own Central Works in Edgbaston, Birmingham and based at Stafford garage. Beyond the next pair of Central coaches is an ex-London Transport RTL and a 1966 Metro-Cammell bodied PD2 from Harper Bros. (Heath Hayes), soon to be taken over by Midland Red. A fifth Central coach can just be seen beyond the two double-deckers. A similar line-up would occur at each shift change at 07.00, 15.00 and 23.00 every weekday.

The major coach operator in Wolverhampton, with more than 70 coaches, was Don Everall Travel. In the 1950s they bought a variety of heavyweight vehicles but eventually became a Ford main dealer and standardised on this make until they sold out to National Travel Midlands in 1974. 1970 Duple Viceroy C53F Ford R226 (AUK 606H) is travelling through Cannock on a contract service from nearby Littleton Colliery. Heavy lorries, such as the one on the left, were a common sight in town centres at this time before relief roads and weight restrictions were introduced. The coach is passing the Pisces which, not surprisingly, was a fish and chip restaurant!

This view of a Midland Red dual-purpose Leyland Leopard shows how much our motorways have changed in the last 30 years. Harper Bros. (Heath Hayes) Ltd introduced a Motorway Express service operating four times daily, Monday to Saturday, from Hednesford and Cannock to Birmingham via the newly opened M6 Midland Link Motorway. When Harper Bros. was taken over by Midland Red it was numbered X98. The route was then extended via Cannock Chase to Rugeley and re-numbered service X31. This unidentified vehicle is running towards Birmingham on a weekday morning at about 11am. Note the lack of traffic! Just beyond the bus is where the M54 now diverges to and from Telford in Shropshire. As traffic increased, the X31 became less reliable, vehicles often travelling in slow-moving nose-to-tail queues for the main part of the motorway section of the route. It was eventually re-routed back to the A34 in the 1980s because it was quicker than using the motorway. The re-opening of the Rugeley-Birmingham railway line was the final nail in the coffin for the X31, which no longer exists. The section of the M6 motorway it covered is now duplicated in part by the new M6 Toll.

Midland Red ordered more than 300 Daimler Fleetline double-deckers between 1963 and 1971, all with Alexander bodies and classed as D11, D12 and D13. In 1976 the final Fleetlines, designated D14, were delivered, a couple of ECW H43/31F CRG6LXs, originally ordered by Harpers of Heath Hayes. The last one of all, No.440 (JOX 440P) is at the Heath Hayes depot still carrying trade plates after delivery from Midland Red Central Works at Carlyle Road in Edgbaston, Birmingham.

Harper Bros. (Heath Hayes) Ltd operated a large number of second-hand buses and these are two of them, away from their normal operating area at Lymers' Tean premises, during an enthusiasts' tour. As the buses crossed the foothills of the Pennines en route from Uttoxeter, they encountered a short, sharp blizzard. The de-misting on the 1951 St Helens RT, No.9, (BDJ 807) is barely adequate as can be seen by the tiny viewing area cleared for the driver through the snowed-up windscreen. This bus had platform doors fitted soon after it came into Harpers' ownership in 1962. No.11 (888 DUK) has faired a little better, with its relatively modern de-misting system. The Strachans bodied H72F, Guy Arab V with semi-automatic gearbox, was known to staff as the 'Old Grey Mare' – due to her low top speed and original demonstrator's off-white livery. Before settling in with Harpers, in 1966, it had toured the UK and worked for various operators, its unique design with heavily raked front and totally square rear, ensuring that it was instantly recognisable to enthusiasts.

After Midland Red Omnibus took over Harper Bros. (Heath Hayes) vehicles soon started travelling to Central Works at Carlyle Road, Birmingham to be repainted in National Bus Company poppy red. The 1968 Northern Counties PD3A/1 on the right, No.2226 (LRF 993F) has just returned from the works and retains its original destination layout. No.23 (NRF 349F), a PD3A/2, was notably the last PD3 to be built for a UK independent operator. When it makes its visit for repaint it will be fitted with standard Midland Red three track number and twin destination blinds, and renumbered 2223. It was also notable in having a high ratio rear axle and when operating empty along the M6 to Birmingham to operate peak-time services, could attain speeds of more than 60 miles per hour – if the Smiths speedometer could be believed. The vehicle on the right is a Duple bodied Bedford VAM, recently repainted in the famous National white coach livery.

This Harpers 1968 Leyland Leopard PSU3/3R with Duple Commander III C51F body was, surprisingly, on a stage carriage service. No.75 (ORF 459F) is en route to Calf Heath from Cannock on a quiet journey with the author in charge (which explains the apparent lack of a driver). Midland Red had recently taken over the operation (in April 1974) as shown by the sticker in the top of the windscreen, but in the interim period before full ownership it continued to maintain the traditional system used by many independents on one man operation. The driver keeps the ticket machine under his seat and hangs the cash bag from any suitable hook or switch. This batch of four vehicles was never converted for one-man operation and all of them were repainted into National white livery, continuing to give service as coaches for several more years.

Whilst Harper Bros. No.30 (JBF 406H) a 1970 Daimler Fleetline CRG6LX with Northern Counties H77F bodywork is well worth admiring, the crowds are actually gathering outside the Co-op to watch the passing of the 1971 Heath Hayes Carnival Procession. Three pairs of Fleetlines were delivered to the company, in 1970, 1971 and 1973, the final pair being ECW bodied CRL6s. The bus has just over an hour's journey ahead of it before arriving in Birmingham Carrs Lane. It is worth noting that although the police are in attendance, there is not one high visibility vest in sight!

The rear view of a Burlingham Seagull coach is just as distinctive as the front, but far less often photographed. Harper Bros. (Heath Hayes) Ltd had a pair of Guy Arab LUF C41F coaches delivered in 1959. They often appeared on their Hednesford-Birmingham Motorway Express route introduced in 1969 just after the M6 Midland Link was opened. This view of No.59 (1293 RE) was taken from another Harpers coach, during a 'Farewell Harpers' route tour on the afternoon of Sunday 21 April 1974. The relatively light traffic on this section of the M6 at Wednesbury, just before the M5 junction, would have been normal for a Sunday afternoon in the early days of the motorway, a far cry from the regular nose-to-tail congestion experienced today. Happily this coach and its sister vehicle, No.60 have both been preserved.

Two of the best-known and largest Staffordshire independent operators were Stevensons of Spath, near Uttoxeter, and Harper Bros. (Heath Hayes) Ltd. Their operating areas did not actually overlap so the opportunity was taken during an enthusiast visit to Stevensons in 1971 to position a pair of ex-London Transport RTLs side by side for this photograph. Stevensons No.29 (KGU 216) still has its LT-style flashing indicators and a destination display featuring just the old final destination blind. Most notable perhaps is the tree-battered front dome, reflecting the rural nature of the routes often operated by this bus. By comparison the Harpers RTL, No.3 (OLD 820) has a much smoother dome profile, and is fitted with contemporary flashers. Another vehicle of interest in the background is the half-cab single-deck 1950 Leyland Tiger PS1/1 with Willowbrook DP35F body, GAY 170, originally operated by Allen of Mountsorrel in Leicestershire.

Stevenson No.10 (564 FTF) a Leyland PD3/4 with a Metro-Cammell H31/42RD body is close to the firm's Burton on Trent garage as it reaches the end of its 15-mile journey from Uttoxeter via Tutbury. This bus was originally owned by Lancashire United Transport as No.647, until purchased by Stevensons in 1971. It is being followed down the almost deserted road by a Dodge delivery van, a name, along with Leyland, which has long ceased manufacturing. The New Inn pub on the right boasts a red Bass triangle, another well-known British trade-mark which has now all but disappeared. The 24-hour cigarette vending machine attached to the shop on the left is also worthy of note.

Warstone Motors operated under their own name in the 1970s but were to become better known as the Green Bus Service of Great Wyrley. This view in 1976 shows No.14 (521 CTF), a 1957 Leyland Olympian in the Staffordshire village of Brewood making its way back to Cannock. The route had recently been taken over from Milestone Coaches of Gailey. This bus was purchased from Williams of Chirk who in turn had bought it from Fishwick of Leyland. In the distance is a Midland Red Daimler Fleetline en route from Wheaton Aston to Wolverhampton on the 878 service. One interesting feature of Warstone's operation was the use of ancient Bell ticket punches and racks more readily associated with historic tramway practice.

Whieldon's Green Bus Company operated from depots in Rugeley and Uttoxeter until take-over by Midland Red in 1973. No.25 (GVH 796) was originally fleet number 6 for the Huddersfield Joint Omnibus Committee before its sale to Green Bus. It is a 1954 Guy Arab UF with Guy/ Park Royal B43F bodywork. It is unusual in having a pre-selective gearbox rather than a crash-box which was the more usual choice for Guy buses. In autumn 1970, the driver can be seen on board preparing the bus in the Uttoxeter depot, ready for its journey to Rugeley and onward to Cannock via The Chase.

H&M Coaches of Chasetown had several coaches and double-deckers, mostly used on contract services. In the late 1960s they bought several Park Royal bodied Guy Arab IVs from a batch originally delivered to East Kent Road Car Company in 1956/7. No.11 (MFN 891) is in the parking area of Lichfield bus station in 1969, waiting to operate a contract service later in the afternoon. Lichfield City station can be seen behind No.11, at that time terminus for the regular Diesel Multiple Unit service to Birmingham.

Churchbridge Coaches was based in Bridgtown, a suburb of Cannock on the major intersection of the A34 and A5 trunk roads. The firm mainly operated coaches but also ran CHD 612, this smart ex-Yorkshire Woollen District AEC Regent V with Metro-Cammell Orion H70F bodywork dating from 1958. The spoil tip in the background shows that coal mining had been a major local industry, but this view is now completely changed, the M6 toll-motorway running right through the site of the former garage.

Middletons of Rugeley ran mainly contract services around this Staffordshire town, so there was no requirement to leave the destination blind visible on this bus, photographed in the operator's yard. They also built up a fleet of several Plaxton bodied AEC Reliances for private-hire work, one of which stands in the background. This ex-Southdown 1956 Leyland PD2/12, RUF 197 with East Lancs H59RD bodywork, is one of many sold for further service to other operators, but not all of them carried a livery that made such a contrast with the original operator's famous green and cream. It came to Middletons via Greatrex of Stafford and was finally withdrawn in September 1973.

6680 KH was a 1960 Metro-Cammell dual-purpose 41 seat Leyland Tiger Cub PSUC1/2. Originally bought by East Yorkshire Motor Services, it was often used on the Hull to Birmingham express service, at that time part of the Yorkshire Services network. It moved next within the British Electric Traction group to United Counties Omnibus Company based in Bedford and they in turn sold it to Carneys of Rugeley in May 1970. It is seen here on a far less taxing route, on the short journey from Springfields in Rugeley to the town centre just a mile away. The low autumnal sun shows this to be a late afternoon trip. The conductor has a chance to chat with his driver before returning to load up in town with shoppers making their way home to this almost new housing estate.

Greatrex Travel Services ran several contract services in the Stafford area, many of them of a rural nature. They acquired a stage carriage service from Stafford to Hixon in 1966 when they took over H Nickolls & Son in 1966. This photograph at their Stone Road premises in Stafford shows recent addition to the fleet VBF 697J, a smartly presented 1971 Ford R192 with Willowbrook DP45F body. The rear of the 1966 Strachans bodied B46F Ford 192 (ARF 873D) is visible to the left. At the time of this photograph the entire fleet of two dozen coaches was standardised on Ford chassis, the majority of which carried coach bodies by Duple.

Shropshire Omnibus Association Ltd (SOA) comprised several independent operators, one of which was Smith's Eagle Coachways of Trench near Wellington. This AEC Reliance, NUX 256, was new to them in 1956 and is fitted with a Burlingham B44F body. This view (about 1969) is close to its base in nearby Donnington. When Midland Red took over the stage carriage services of the SOA this early-model underfloor-engined single-deck bus did not pass to the new operator.

Sentinel buses were never a common sight as only 125 were built for the UK market. H Brown & Sons of Donnington Wood continued to operate a small fleet of them later than any other operator, the last being withdrawn in 1973. Possibly this was because of local Shropshire loyalty, the Sentinel works being only a few miles away in the county town of Shrewsbury. JUJ 264, a Sentinel STC/40, is in the Brown's depot alongside a more modern Bedford SB5. Several of Brown's Sentinels were preserved and survive at the time of writing, although this one was not so lucky and was scrapped at the depot in 1971.

F Proctor & Son of Hanley purchased 4559 VC from Daimler in 1964 after it had spent two years as a demonstrator. It is an early Daimler Fleetline CRG6LX with a Northern Counties body and is on the route 16 from Leek to Hanley passing the premises of another well-known Staffordshire operator, Berresfords of Cheddleton. With the success of this purchase, Proctors went on to buy two more new Fleetlines. They remain one the few original Potteries independents to be operating in the 21st century. Berresfords would eventually be bought out by Potteries Motor Traction in 1987. The red single-deck bus on the right is an ex-Southdown Leyland Tiger Cub PSUC1/1 with Duple Midland B39F bodywork.

W Stonier & Sons of Goldenhill in the Potteries favoured second-hand Leyland double-deck buses. This pair is seen outside their cramped depot in 1971. The front entrance Massey bodied PD2 (961 GBF) on the left had a relatively short move from Turners of Brown Edge, an operator just five miles away, whilst the lowbridge Northern Counties bodied Leyland PD2 (RVA 763) had originally been operated by Hutchinson's Coaches of Overtown in Lanarkshire, over 200 miles away.

Harrington of Hove in Sussex was a well-known coach builder. A feature of many of their coaches was the dorsal fin, first developed in the 1930s. This gives an exciting, modern look, although its main function is to provide additional ventilation as can clearly be seen on this rear-view of URE 281. This example was built in 1950 on an AEC Regal III chassis for Lymers of Tean, between Stoke on Trent and Uttoxeter. An additional feature of this coach is its contemporary full front, unfortunately not visible in this view. Although now preserved it was still with its original owners when photographed during a depot visit in the early 1970s.

Potteries Motor Traction (PMT) was a British Electric Traction group operator, absorbed into the National Bus Company in 1969. They had always operated coaches as well as buses; some were bought new while many were acquired as PMT took over other operators. This Harrington C41F Leyland Leopard No.23 (PCK 602) had been previously operated by Standerwick, part of Ribble Motor Services, and was run from 1972 to 1976 by PMT. It is in Derby bus station, taking a break while on private hire. The blue double-decker to the left is a Derby City Transport Daimler Fleetline with a Roe body.

Turner was an independent operator based in Brown Edge to the north of the Potteries. They operated a small fleet of coaches and buses with about half a dozen double-deckers available for their stage-carriage service to Hanley, four miles away. KRE 266B, a 1964 Leyland PD2 at the firm's depot, has a very traditional look in 1971 with its Massey bodywork and exposed radiator, but would soon be replaced by a Daimler Fleetline. The firm was taken over by Potteries Motor Traction in 1988 and the livery was perpetuated for several years on buses run by the new owners.

Within a few years of the Second World War, most single-deck buses were built with underfloor engines and front entrances although they always carried a conductor at that time. Burton on Trent Corporation, No.63 (FA 9291) a 1949 Guy Arab III 5LW, therefore looks particularly dated with its half-cab and rear entrance Guy B35R bodywork. It is standing at the back of their depot towards the end of its life. Most other operators had withdrawn such vehicles by the time this photograph was taken in 1971.

Burton on Trent Corporation Transport Daimler Fleetline CRG6LX No.106 (RFA 406J) with Northern Counties H42/33F body in its home town in 1972, alongside Wetmore bus station and carrying its original maroon and white livery. The bus is being pursued by a BMC FG lorry. In the background is one of the many huge maltings so typical of this famous brewing town. Soon after this photograph was taken, the fleet was renamed East Staffordshire District Council and by 1975 the buses were re-painted in red, white and green.

Burton on Trent Corporation built up a large fleet of lightweight double-decker Guys and Daimlers with Gardner 5 cylinder engines, so it was something of a contrast when they bought a pair of heavyweight 1954 Leyland Royal Tiger PSU1/13s with Burlingham B42F bodywork from Bournemouth Corporation Transport in 1971. No.1 (NLJ 271) was at the outer terminus of the 7 service. It carried the new livery of green, white and red recently introduced by the manager, Roy Marshall, replacing the more traditional maroon and cream. They were bought so that one-man operation could be introduced to the town. More second-hand buses from the south coast were to follow in the form of Portsmouth City Leyland Atlanteans. On the far right Tony Peart, the well known transport enthusiast, can be seen preparing his tape recorder ready to record the sound effects of No.1 on its return journey to the town centre.

Tailby and George, trading as Blue Bus of Willington, were well known for their fleet of immaculate double-deckers operating between Burton on Trent and Derby. They also ran a small coach fleet which in later years was made up of Bedford lightweights. This splendid Duple C35F bodied Daimler CVD6 is still operational in this late 1960s view, outside the firm's depot. Fortunately the coach was withdrawn and sold for preservation and escaped the devastating fire that destroyed so many vehicles in 1976. It still survives in the 21st century.

Two immaculate Blue Bus of Willington Daimler Fleetline CRG6LXs are seen in Wetmore bus station in Burton on Trent in 1972. On the left is JRB 481D with a Northern Counties body new in 1996 and on the right is NRA 49J, new in 1971, and carrying an Alexander body. As the destination blinds indicate, there are two totally different trunk routes to Derby, just over ten miles away. In December 1973 ownership of the company was transferred to Derby Corporation Transport. Sadly both these buses, along with several others, were destroyed in the tragic Willington garage fire in January 1976.

City of Oxford Motor Services (COMS) had a reputation for well-maintained buses and their second-hand AECs were much sought-after by independent operators. 953 AJO, a Weymann H61R bodied AEC Regent V, is in Derby bus station having been sold to Parkin of Borrowash, trading as Luxicoaches of Derby. It was used mainly on contract services. The very traditional style of livery, with five different bands of red and cream, enhances the stark lines of the Orion bodywork even if it is not as striking as COMS original maroon, red and duck egg blue. One cannot help but think that 'Luxicoaches' is something of a misnomer, though for most enthusiasts the AEC sound effects would more than compensate for the basic seats!

The centrepiece of this 1969 view of Nottingham Broad Marsh bus station is a 1947 Barton Transport Leyland PD1 with Duple L55F bodywork No.468 (JRR 751). This layout of bodywork with a forward entrance and offside sunken gangway was relatively unusual around the country, yet Barton ran over 50 double-deckers built to this specification. In between the two buses can be seen Barton's wooden booking office with three different designs of sign, advertising the company's name. Above the office on the right is the Great Central Railway Weekday Cross Junction and beyond that are buildings around the Lace Market where, since March 2004, state of the art Nottingham Express Transit (NET) trams have been running. The advert on the side of the bus is for the local Shipstone's brewery, which would eventually close in 1991. Times change; in the car park every identifiable car is of British manufacture, including a Ford Cortina, an Austin Cambridge and two BMC Minis.

Barton Transport Ltd operated 300 vehicles from ten different garages in the East Midlands and became known amongst enthusiasts for operating an amazing collection of second-hand and re-bodied buses. This 1969 view at Long Eaton depot shows a typical pair of vehicles with modern bodies powered by ancient running units. No.798 (798 BAL) is a 1958 re-build with a low-bridge Northern Counties body seating 63 passengers. Classified as a PS1/B, this bus originally ran as a single-deck Leyland Tiger. No.904 (904 LRR) looks similar but can seat 70 passengers and is built on a chassis that came from Yorkshire Woollen District in 1961. It is registered by Barton as a BTD2, as effectively, after re-building, it has become a new bus.

No.267 (XTO 267) a 1956 Park Royal H62R bodied AEC Regent V, leads a trio of Nottingham City Transport (NCT) buses past the new Broad Marsh shopping centre in 1971. Behind the red Hillman Avenger is No.46 (46 NAU) the first ever NCT rear-engined bus, a 1962 Park Royal H77F Daimler Fleetline CRG6LX. This was to be followed by nearly 200 more Daimler Fleetlines over the next fifteen years along with a similar number of Leyland Atlanteans. Deliveries after 1964 were fitted with Nottingham's own distinctive body style. Bringing up the rear is another AEC Regent V, from the XTO batch.

The South Notts Bus Company Ltd was based at Gotham a few miles south of Nottingham, until it was sold to Nottingham City Transport in 1991. Many of their services used to terminate at the old outdoor Broad Marsh bus station which had recently been closed and replaced by a new bus station under a car park. This photograph was taken soon after the new complex opened in October 1971; No.48 (MRR 338) a 1951 all-Leyland L53R PD2/12, is parked ahead of No.70 (670 BNN) a Leyland PD3/3 dating from 1958 with its unusual Weymann Aurora L67R body.

West Bridgford Urban District Council (WBUDC) was well known for its attractive and immaculate fleet of AECs, operating from West Bridgford on the south side of the River Trent into Nottingham Old Market Square and Broadmarsh Bus Station. No.6 (KAL 686) an AEC Regent III with Park Royal H31/25R body from 1949 is seen here with driver and conductor conferring at the outer terminus of route 14 before returning to Nottingham. This view was taken on Saturday 21 December 1968, a few weeks after the take-over of WBUDC by Nottingham City Transport on 21 September. The West Bridgford coat of arms and initials have been removed from the side of the bus. The vehicle is in a much dirtier condition than would have been permitted before the sale. It will be noted that some 20 years after railway nationalisation, one of the destinations on the blind is 'LMS Station'!

East Midland Motor Services, part of the British Electric Traction Group (BET), was based in Chesterfield and operated as far north as Doncaster and Sheffield, beyond the area that the fleet-name would suggest. In the 1950s it had a drastic livery change, from mustard, brown and cream to a somewhat drab maroon and cream. This is the livery seen on No.521 (PNN 521F) a 1968 Bristol RE with ECW B49F bodywork and an early MkI Leyland Atlantean No.154 (154 HRR), outside the Worksop combined garage and bus station in the early 1970s. This was just after the BET Group had become part of the National Bus Company. The ECW-bodied RE had a good reputation as a rugged and reliable bus. East Midlands bought a batch as soon as the restriction which had limited sales to the Tilling group of bus companies was lifted. This restriction was introduced following the 1947 Transport Act which allowed Bristol chassis and Eastern Coach Works bodies only to be sold to companies which were under state ownership – an extraordinary provision it seems now. The National Bus Company brought a further livery change to NBC green as can be seen to the extreme left on another Atlantean.

Leicester City Transport bought 65 Leyland bodied PD2s in 1949/50. No.105 (FJF 144) H60R was the last of the 10 delivered in 1949. It is in Charles Street, Leicester by the W A Lea's building, on Saturday 28 October 1967, just after working the infrequent 56 service from the Towers Hospital. This route operated to coincide with hospital visiting times only: Thursday, Saturday and Sunday afternoons. Two months after this, the bus was withdrawn from service and in the following February it was sold to Margo's Coaches of Bexleyheath.

Leicester City Transport No.195 (ABC 195B) was the first bus in the fleet to carry a year suffix letter and was one of a pair of AEC Reliance 4MU3RAs delivered in April 1964. It is in Charles Street, Leicester, in November 1967; the buildings are still much the same but traffic schemes have drastically altered the road layout. The Marshall bodywork originally had just a front-entrance and 54 seats but No.195 had been converted to B50D layout the previous June. It was to be sold to Colchester Corporation in 1971; they converted it back to single-door, B53F layout, just one month after purchase.

This view is still recognisable today although the names of the buildings have changed. No.220 (220 DRY) a Leicester City Transport AEC Bridgemaster with H45/31R Park Royal bodywork, is loading in Halford Street prior to working the 67 route to Evington. The driver is negotiating his way through the cab door. In the distance, at the far end of Rutland Street, is the classic 1930s Art Deco Odeon cinema, now a popular venue called The Athena. Immediately behind the two buses is the Queens hostelry, which has since been taken over by the Hoskins family and is now one of Leicester's premier real ale pubs, The Ale Wagon.

Leicester City Transport purchased their first three rear-engined buses in 1963. One of these, a Leyland Atlantean PDR1/1, is on the left, No.187 (187 DRY) fitted with a Metro-Cammell H77F body. The Transport Department was obviously not wholly impressed with the concept as they went back to buying another 83 half-cab, front-engined buses in the next four years. Seventy of these were rear-entrance Leyland PD3s and the other thirteen were AEC Renowns. In 1968 they finally bought another twenty Leyland Atlantean PDR1A/1s, the first ten with ECW bodies and the rest with Park Royal H74F bodies. The last of the batch No.115 (PBC 115G) is inside the Abbey Park Road depot in 1972. This was the first all-over advertisement bus in the fleet and had its number plate placed in a non-standard position for LCT, below the manufacturer's badge rather than above the windscreen. The depot first opened in 1904 to house over 150 trams and was subsequently converted for buses. Ownership was transferred to Grampian Regional Transport in 1993 and then to First Group in 1995. It closed in 2007 after more than a hundred years, replaced by a new depot half a mile away at Abbey Lane.

Leicester City Transport had a large fleet of PD3s built up between 1958 and 1968, eventually totalling one hundred and seventeen. These vehicles featured bodies by different builders and No.166 (TBC 166) was one of an unusual trio delivered with Willowbrook H41/33R coachwork from nearby Loughborough. It is seen in High Street, Leicester, in 1973 carrying the cream livery that has replaced the maroon in which it was originally delivered in 1958. Relatively little of the townscape hereabouts has changed since. Even the same PUKKA PIE sign hangs outside the fish and chip shop. The Morris Minor pick-up heading out of town is about to meet an Austin A55 van whilst a Ford Anglia van makes a delivery to the left of the bus. It is doubtful whether many suited businessmen wearing trilby hats would be in evidence today!

In 1949 Northampton Corporation Transport purchased ten Daimler CVG6s with Roe rear-entrance bodies and open platforms. This combination was purchased in 15 batches over the next 30 years. The final batch of six was delivered in 1968, culminating with the now-preserved No.267 (JVV 267G). The photograph, taken on a quiet afternoon in the Drapery in the summer of 1974, shows four similar buses from at least two different batches. On the right is No.266 (JVV 266G) the penultimate bus of this type. To the left is the rear of No.245 (SVV 245) the last of the batch of six buses delivered in 1964. It is a warm and sunny afternoon and most of the pedestrians are in light, informal summer clothing. Close inspection of the rear upstairs emergency door of No.245 shows an unusual feature of Northampton's buses. On such a warm day the emergency door could be locked in a slightly open position, allowing air to flow straight through the upper saloon.

G&G Coaches of Leamington Spa operated an interesting selection of buses on contract services. JUE 348 has made a relatively short move from its original operator, Stratford Blue, just a few miles to the west. Originally built in 1950 as a single-deck Willowbrook-bodied Leyland PS2/3, it was rebuilt in 1963 as a double-decker with Northern Counties H35/28F body. Just behind can be seen an AEC Regent V of the KTG batch originally delivered to Rhondda Transport Company in 1961. To the left is a viaduct carrying the old Great Western Railway line from Paddington to Birmingham Snow Hill. It was possible to view the interesting fleet below while travelling across the viaduct on northbound trains.

Finally, on the very edge of the Midlands, Cheltenham District was part of the Bristol Omnibus Company but operated as a separate unit. The buses were painted in a non-standard maroon and cream livery unlike any other in the Tilling Group, which were mainly painted red or green. They also had the town coat of arms under the fleet-name. On an April afternoon in 1972 the driver, conductor and inspector are waiting optimistically for a rush of passengers to the racecourse, with No.L97 (YHT 964) a 1957 Bristol Lodekka LD (ECW H58R bodywork). Note also the interesting collection of cars parked on the forecourt of the office block just behind the bus.